# Alexander Hamilton:

*by Ron Chernow* |

Summary & Highlights

## Authored By

# Summary Reads

# FREE GIFT SPECIAL REPORT

## The 10 Strange Deaths of Vladimir Putin

While History is filled with intrigue, war posturing, bribes and assassinations our current day is just as filled (if not more) with exciting (if not terrifying) but true stories.

As our **free gift** for being a **SUMMARY READS enthusiast** we are happy to give you a special report about some of the mysterious and <u>strange deaths</u> that have befallen Mr. Putin's enemies.

Plane crashes, multiple stab wounds and radioactive sushi are just a few of the misfortunes that have befallen those who opposed the Russian President.

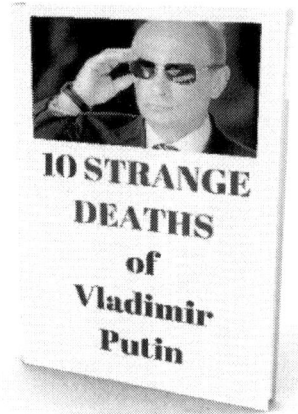

Get your free copy at:

## http://sixfigureteen.com/summaryreads

<u>ALSO</u>: We will let you know about future Summary Reads titles so this is win-win! Enjoy your FREE GIFT and thank you for being part of the SUMMARY READS Family!

**ISBN-10:** 1522904123
**ISBN-13:** 978-1522904120

# DISCLAIMERS

- Absolutely nothing in this volume is meant to constitute legal, financial, or medical advice nor are the opinions presented to be considered expert opinions.
- This volume is **NOT** meant to be a replacement for the original book; we believe our summation, key quotes and highlight analysis will increase interest in the complete book and not detract from it.
- **No historians were hurt** in the writing, editing and publishing of this volume.
- In this volume, each particular detail is presented to the best of our knowledge and understanding of the popular book about Alexander Hamilton. If you think any of our analysis or summation is inaccurate **please email us** and we will correct it and publish an updated edition after verifying (levelproperty@gmail.com).
- Most importantly: absolutely no portion of this summation volume was written in a Starbucks.

# CONTENTS

# Alexander Hamilton – *SINGLE PAGE SUMMARY*

This story of Alexander Hamilton details a true story of an American Revolutionary war hero that was a true founding father. Hamilton was born in disarray in the British West Indies. He escaped a life of meaninglessness and moved to New York as a teenager where he set his feet in political and military prowess.

Over the years he worked with the greatest leaders in American history. He was the chief of staff to General Washington in the Revolutionary War and his Secretary of the Treasury in his two presidential terms.

Hamilton was a man that deeply cared for his family and his duty. Even into his death he maintained a sense of responsibility future generations should take note of.

# CHAPTER SUMMARY 1: THE CASTAWAYS
## (SUMMARY/HIGHLIGHTS & BEST QUOTES)

Alexander Hamilton was born in the British West Indies island of Nevis. The British West Indies is gloriously beautiful in natural wonder and horrific in treachery all at the same time.

Some would say that Nevis was a sleepy backwater location for a larger than life future American leader, but with the bitter maritime rivalries fought in its seas and the lucrative sugar trade it was far from a marginal birthplace.

The, seemingly, overnight popularity of sugar, given the moniker "white gold" made slavery indispensable in the eyes of the sugar plantation owners in Nevis and the other British West Indies.

Hamilton's family fell in the insecure middle class that was stuck between the aristocrats running the plantations and the band of slaves they ruled.

There is a certain mythology about Hamilton's mother's, Rachel, race. Some believe her to be part black, causing Hamilton to be a black descent as well. There is no veritable facts supporting this, she was listed on tax documents as white. Most likely this rose from the fact that Hamilton was an illegitimate child and most illegitimate children born in the British West Indies at this time bore mixed blood.

Rachel left her husband, Lavien, around 1750 and he immediately started a campaign to make her appear as a prostitute, thus, illegitimatizing all her children. One critic of Hamilton wrote that he was the son of a "camp girl." In an effort to humiliate her, Rachel's husband had her jailed for cheating on him.

After release from jail Rachel fled to the island of St. Kitts in 1750. Rachel met James Hamilton in the early 1750s on St. Kitts. Divorce was never easy in these times and she was never free from Lavien. She and James maintained a common-law marriage that produced two children: James Jr. and Alexander.

## Best Quote?

*"The West Indies vastly outweigh us of the northern colonies."*

*"My birthplace is the subject of the most humiliating criticism"*

*"Solitude had only stiffened her resolve to expel Lavien from her life."*

*"It's a dog of a life when two dissonant tempers meet."*

YOU DECIDE: **@SummaryReads**

# CHAPTER SUMMARY 2: HURRICANE
## (SUMMARY/HIGHLIGHTS & BEST QUOTES)

Hamilton's first job, a clerk, offered him valuable insights into global commerce and the maneuvers of imperial powers. Beekman and Cruger, the company in which he worked, offered him a direct link to New York City. St. Croix had a trading arrangement with many companies in New York and this would eventually lead Hamilton to take up residence in the State.

Hamilton lost his parents, but that did not cease his desire to be great. Hamilton had a goal, liberation for St. Croix, and that was never easy when you were not born into aristocracy. Alexander Hamilton had to earn everything he would achieve.

Hamilton's work allotted him to many extensive understandings of trade and countries working together, which eventually, led to his establishment of the U.S. Coast Guard and Customs Service.

By the time Hamilton had grown the slave population of St. Croix had doubled in just a decade. The idea of insurrection plagued the plantation owners so much so that they set up guard to keep slaves from fleeing to Puerto Rico, a Spanish colony.

This unsettling climate made St. Croix a brutal place to live. An insurgent slave would be castrated and then hung or beheaded to serve as a warning to other like-minded slaves.

One cannot fully understand Hamilton's later politics without understanding the raw cruelty that he witnessed as a boy and that later deprived him of hopefulness so contagious in the American milieu.

## Best Quote?

*"Ambitioned orphaned boys do not enjoy the option of idleness."*

*"Punishments were designed to be hellish so as to terrorize the rest of the captive population into submission."*

*"If a slave lifted a hand in resistance, it would promptly be chopped off."*

*"The twin specters of despotism and anarchy were to haunt him for the rest of his life."*

YOU DECIDE: **@SummaryReads**

# CHAPTER SUMMARY 3: THE COLLEGIAN
## (SUMMARY/HIGHLIGHTS & BEST QUOTES)

A middle-class man from the British West Indies would have lots of social hurdles to maneuver in order to gain any semblance of success.

Hamilton was able to do this with ease. He was a gregarious individual that enlisted his smarts and good looks to help him gain ground in his newfound world of New York.

He attended Elizabethtown Academy in New Jersey. His schooling here placed him in the path of a lifelong acquaintance, Aaron Burr.

Hamilton had a knack to impress those of high class and as he grew into his new surroundings, high-class leaders found him and took him in. One such man to take Hamilton under his wing was William Livingston.

The Livingston household was full of future leaders in the new America. Livingston's oldest daughter, Sarah, was betrothed to a young lawyer and future Supreme Court Justice, John Jay. But Hamilton had his eye on another daughter, Kitty. In the end Kitty married William Duer, the most notorious friend in Hamilton's life.

Hamilton also befriended Elias Boudinot, future president of the Continental Congress. He would regularly visit the Boudinot Mansion and there became acquainted with a large world of books, political debate, and high culture.

Both Boudinot and Livingston sat on Princeton's Board of Trustees, yet another sign that the middle-class Hamilton was learning how to connect to the upper and high classes of the northern colonies.

Hamilton had a desire to go through Princeton with as much "rapidity" as possible. However, the new President of Princeton found that and his age, 17, a major hindrance to acceptance. Most at this time were entering college at 14 or 15 and this proved that Hamilton wasn't from a high-class consortium.

While he was fighting his way out of the islands, aristocrats were entering college. He had two choices lie about his age or attend another school. He chose to attend King's College.

## Best Quote?

*"I want to enter the college and advance with as much rapidity as possible."*

YOU DECIDE: **@SummaryReads**

# CHAPTER SUMMARY 4: THE PEN AND THE SWORD
## (SUMMARY/HIGHLIGHTS & BEST SIZZLE/STEAK QUOTES)

As 1775 rolled around revolution was in the air. Hamilton joined the uniformed companies of militia that were now springing up around the colonies. The same persistent attitude he espoused with his studies he took to the military field as well.

During this time a mob of revolutionists began to attack King's College and its President. Hamilton hears of this uprising and tries to explain to the crowd that this was not the correct way to go about it.

The president didn't realize Hamilton was trying to help him and he began to incite the crowd telling them not to believe a word Hamilton said. Hamilton held the crowd off long enough for the disgraced president to escape. The two never saw each other again and the president was heard in despair when he learned that America had won the war.

Hamilton got his first taste of the Britain war machine in August of 1776. He was in Manhattan and the Britain's were attacking by sea. He and fifteen other King's College volunteers bravely saved the fort's artillery amidst a barrage of cannonball fire by England.

Hamilton also went to pen and paper to fight for his beliefs. According to letters sent to St. Croix and to address others in New York he clearly favored revolution, but feared that disorderly conduct would continue long after the war.

Still his papers and other writings were a major help to the war cause, rallying untold amounts of militia men to the American cause.

## Best Quote?

*"Hamilton was constant in his attendance and very ambitious of improvement."*

*"The injury you have done to your country cannot admit of reparation."*

*"Don't mind anything Hamilton says. He's a little fool."*

## CHAPTER SUMMARY 5: THE LITTLE LION

### (SUMMARY/HIGHLIGHTS & BEST QUOTES)

As the war drug on Washington became increasingly more aware of the brave prowess of Alexander Hamilton. Hamilton saved Washington's men in a retreat in New York that allowed them to get out safely and Washington told Congress about the bravery of Hamilton and the sense he had about him in perilous times.

As Hamilton earned the honor of artillery captain he led his men through difficult conditions and illnesses and earned the respect of everyone in which he came into contacted. Many remarked at his youthfulness and bravery beyond his years.

All his hard work paid off when he was asked to join Washington's team as an aide-de-camp. In less than five years Hamilton had risen from despondent clerk in St. Croix to one of the aides to American's most eminent men.

However, Hamilton balked at this opportunity because it would take him out of the battlefield and chain him to a desk. However, he took the assignment and it led to many different political connections that would aid him in the future.

Hamilton proved to be indispensible to Washington as he freed Washington up to get on the front lines knowing his letters to Congress and others were in good hands. He evolved from a secretary of some sorts to the chief of staff for Washington. Some of his duties:

- Rode with the general into combat
- Cantered off on diplomatic missions
- Dealt with generals
- Sorted through intelligence files
- Dealt with deserters
- Negotiated prisoner exchanges

## Best Quote?

*"At their head was a boy and I wondered at his youth, but to my surprise it was Hamilton the man we have already heard so much about."*

YOU DECIDE: @SummaryReads

# CHAPTER SUMMARY 6: A FRENZY OF VALOR

## (SUMMARY/HIGHLIGHTS & BEST QUOTES)

In 1788 the outlook for the Americans was bleak at best. Hamilton, off mandatory rest from a debilitating illness, makes it to the camp of Washington and is shocked to see such dire circumstances.

Washington and Hamilton had somewhat of a feud going on. Hamilton longed to be on the frontlines leading troops to battle, while; Washington could not stand the loss of his most trusted aide.

It was Hamilton that penned important letters to Congress demanding they meet the needs of the men and Washington knew he did not have time for these matters nor could he trust anyone, other than Hamilton, with these issues.

Hamilton is given some charge in defeating the enemy and communicating with Washington's generals. One general was given the charge to attack the red coats and slow them until Washington could arrive at the battlefield.

Hamilton rides on ahead and finds the general and his troops retreating. He finds the general and demands he turn around and goes as far to say that he will die with him.

Washington bravely, and legendarily, chased down the British and won victory in Monmouth. Upon victory he ordered General Charles Lee court-martialed. As Hamilton hoped to see him punished, Aaron Burr sympathized with Lee.

Burr seemed to always have an issue with the leadership of George Washington and sought to bring those problems to light any way he could.

## Best Quote?

*"For some days past there has been little less than a famine in the camp."*

*"Exert yourself upon this occasion. Our distress is infinite."*

*"Stand fast, my boys, and receive your enemy."*

*"Let us all die rather than retreat…"*

YOU DECIDE: **@SummaryReads**

# CHAPTER SUMMARY 7: THE LOVESICK COLONEL

## (SUMMARY/HIGHLIGHTS & BEST QUOTES)

As France's allying with the new United States caused the war to be more handily won Hamilton moved his sights to life after war. He wanted a wife.

He wrote a letter to a friend stating his requirements for a woman. In it he stated he cared not for her political beliefs because he knew he would win her over with his arguments.

In the winter of 1780 Hamilton met Elizabeth Schuyler. After a month of courting the two decided to wed. He writes Elizabeth a letter detailing why she is a fine woman. This list was an exact replica of the list he had sent his friend just a few months before.

## Best Quote?

*"Hamilton is a gone man."*

YOU DECIDE: **@SummaryReads**

# CHAPTER SUMMARY 8: GLORY
## (SUMMARY/HIGHLIGHTS & BEST QUOTES)

As the war ended Washington and Hamilton go their separate ways. Washington and Hamilton had been at odds over a few differences of opinions and now Hamilton was ready to get back to full-time military service.

In a letter to Washington he states that if he had not accepted the secretary position on Washington's staff he would have raised much faster in rank and that is why he is being over looked on a few certain positions available. Washington is furious at this statement.

As he waited for military assignment Hamilton continued creating connections that extended far beyond the skills of a middle-class boy from St. Croix. He set his sights on superintendent of finances for the new United States.

In the end he lost his nomination because of the support of Robert Morris and George Washington saying he never discussed finances with Hamilton so he had no idea whether he would be a good fit.

Losing the nomination did not deter Hamilton. He wrote a letter to Morris asking to be on his staff and began showing his skill in the form of finance.

He urged the U.S. to create and maintain a National Bank and brilliantly show that the richest of countries use this type of bank to generate revenue and spur private economical gain.

He knew that if we did not secure our finances Britain would soon be back to owning the U.S. by military might or by loans.

## Best Quote?

*"To by this alone she now menaces our independence."*

YOU DECIDE: **@SummaryReads**

# CHAPTER SUMMARY 9: RAGING BILLOWS

## (SUMMARY/HIGHLIGHTS & BEST QUOTES)

In 1782 the nomadic Hamilton began to settle down. He welcomes his infant son, Philip, to the world and sets up home in the Schuyler mansion in Albany, even becoming a permanent New York State citizen.

He ended his war days and began working on the law degree he put on hold for the Revolutionary War. In those days a lawyer had to have a three-year apprenticeship before appearing in court.

Aaron Burr had submitted a request for that rule to be waived for returning veterans and Hamilton sought to make that his goal as well. Six months after he started teaching himself law he passed the bar and was ready for court.

Burr and Hamilton both rushed to set up law offices in the Albany area. It was widely known that war heroes, they both were, would get the lion's share of work in New York.

Hamilton began focusing on taxes and the need for more federal regulation. By now the Continental Congress had to print paper money and borrow from other countries to successfully run the American government.

Hamilton wrote a series of essays that focused on Robert Morris creating enough influence, state to state, that the federal government would receive tax revenues in time and in their entirety.

Hamilton and his friend John Laurens knew that America would only be united by a political crusade to create a republic. After being appointed to Congress Hamilton implored Laurens to join him in Congress and help fight to make the republic a reality. However, prior to reading that letter from Hamilton, Laurens was struck down by British forces, the last remaining in the liberated colonies.

## Best Quote?

*"You cannot imagine how entirely domestic I am growing."*

*"Hamilton qualified for this exemption and set about mastering the law in short order."*

*"Quit your sword my friend, put on the toga, come to Congress…"*

YOU DECIDE: **@SummaryReads**

# CHAPTER SUMMARY 10: A GRAVE, SILENT, STRANGE SORT OF ANIMAL
## (SUMMARY/HIGHLIGHTS & BEST QUOTES)

As soon as Hamilton passed the bar he was flooded with requests from prominent and wealthy men to take their boys under his wing and teach them law. His list was extensive and included the son of John Adams.

Hamilton was considered an honest man and only represented people he believed were innocent. One occasion he chose to deviate from this principle. He won the case but regretted it for the rest of his life.

Hamilton was regarded as a premier lawyer in the early republic. Judge Ambrose Spencer felt like he was the finest of fine men in this country.

As his career flourished a "good-natured" legal rivalry arose between him and Aaron Burr. Many unusual coincidences stamped the lives of Hamilton and Burr. Burr was born wealthy and in the upper colonies while Hamilton was from the islands and born into a stuck middle-class. Yet somehow these two paths would always cross.

Even in the war Hamilton was listed as a founding father. Like Washington, Jefferson, Franklin, Adams and others Hamilton had copious amounts of papers he left behind talking about the war.

Burr is sometimes considered among the founding fathers, but his letters were far less extensive and far less visionary about the war.

## Best Quote?

*"Hamilton was so entirely the friend of his friends… that his power over their affections was entire and lasted through his life."*

*"The greatest man this country ever produced."*

*"Always been opposed in politics but always on good terms…"*

*"Burr seemed interested in only politics."*

YOU DECIDE: **@SummaryReads**

# CHAPTER SUMMARY 11: GHOSTS
## (SUMMARY/HIGHLIGHTS & BEST QUOTES)

The Hamilton's had eight children in their 20-year marriage, thus causing Eliza to be pregnant or rearing a small child for the duration of their marriage. Hamilton was a man known to have a few mistresses and many believed this was the reason why.

Eliza always maintained her husband's stances on politics and caused his political enemies to be her enemies. She was a devout Presbyterian woman that taught her children the Bible. Though Hamilton was baptized he never fully attended church consistently.

He fell into the deistic view of God that he was not present in daily fares, but was still God. This was a view held by many founding fathers at the time. However, he did offer his services to the church for free legal work and rented pew 92 at their local church.

Though he was absent most of the time on business the Hamilton children have no record of ever stating one negative thing about their father, even in private letters.

Interestingly Hamilton struggled to maintain friendships from the past. Hugh Knox, a mentor from St. Croix, complained that he heard from Hamilton during the war but after the war seemed to be an afterthought to Hamilton.

## Best Quote?

*"He never doubted God's existence, embracing Christianity as a system of morality and cosmic justice."*

*"These McKinley fellows have almost taken our breath away by the enthusiasm they manifest for their candidate."*

## CHAPTER SUMMARY 12: AUGUST AND RESPECTABLE ASSEMBLY
## (SUMMARY/HIGHLIGHTS & BEST QUOTES)

Post-Revolution New York saw a flush of prosperity that quickly faded before vanishing altogether in 1785. Hamilton felt that the only way to keep New York and the other new states was to vote in those concerned with the security of American prosperity into positions that can do something about it.

Meanwhile John Adams was issuing a warning to be careful because the most important post-war item on the American agenda is to be the creation of the government. This government would determine if the rebels would stay united as thirteen states interconnected or separate and create their own veritable city-states.

One issue that the new country faced was slavery. James Madison remarked that during the debates over what kind of governing body to utilize for America the underlying problem as slavery. States were not split large and small, they were split north and south, slave and free.

### Best Quote?

*"The most important... and delicate business of the postwar years would be the creation of a central government."*

YOU DECIDE: **@SummaryReads**

# CHAPTER SUMMARY 13: PUBLIUS
## (SUMMARY/HIGHLIGHTS & BEST QUOTES)

As the Revolution brought unity to the colonies the Constitutional Convention did the opposite. The convention turned ugly, divisive, and overtly polarizing.

Given the massive opposition by Virginia and New York, the largest states, the Constitution had an uphill battle for ratification.

One objection to keep American from turning into England was the insistence of a Bill of Rights and the mandatory rotation of presidents. Some felt that a united government would become a dictatorship and that was not something many would be willing to submit under.

One determined antagonist was New York Governor George Clinton. Hamilton went straight for Clinton writing anonymous papers attacking Clinton and his personal and political beliefs.

George Clinton fought back by attacking Hamilton and his mixed-racial and Creole heritage of the British West Indies. He started calling Hamilton Tom Shit. This ignited the racial and social tension that plagued Hamilton and the very thing he tried to escape from when he left the islands.

Hamilton began writing the, now famous, *Federalist Papers*. In time these papers became the foundation for the

Constitution and the beginning of political parties.

Hamilton was the chief editor and creator of the Federalist project and now **The Federalist Papers** is considered a political and literary masterpiece.

## Best Quote?

*"This Constitution is a monster with open mouth and monstrous teeth ready to devour all before it."*

*"That it is on the whole the greatest book dealing with practical politics."*

*"His eloquence… seemed to require opposition to give its full force."*

YOU DECIDE: **@SummaryReads**

# CHAPTER SUMMARY 14: PUTTING THE MACHINE IN MOTION

## (SUMMARY/HIGHLIGHTS & BEST QUOTES)

As the Constitutional period of the United States began, America needed a president with impeachable integrity. He would be the face, forever, of the new republic. Most that accepted the new Constitution did so only because of the thought that George Washington would be its first President.

John Adams returns from Europe in 1788 stating that anything below vice president was beneath. Hamilton knew the whole experiment hinged on Washington being president.

Longtime political enemy, Governor George Clinton decides to run for president and Hamilton had a recurring fear that Clinton would undermine the new government. Clinton had been an attacker of the Constitution from its inception.

## Best Quote?

*"The blame (from failure) will in all probability be laid of the system itself."*

*"Everybody is aware of that defect in the constitution, which renders it possible the man intended for vice president, may , in fact, turn up president."*

YOU DECIDE: @SummaryReads

# CHAPTER SUMMARY 15: VILLAINOUS BUSINESS

## (SUMMARY/HIGHLIGHTS & BEST QUOTES)

Washington is elected as the first President of the United States of America and quickly tabs Hamilton as the Director of the Treasury. Like all in Washington's cabinet Hamilton had the difficult task of creating a job and office team from nothing.

Hamilton, always a hard worker, employed no one but himself to write his speeches and articles. Also Hamilton had to devise rudimentary systems for bookkeeping, checking, and auditing. Many of these systems survived several generations before updates were warranted.

As his political life was nearing its apex Hamilton found his desire to be with his family was growing deeper by the day. He would write Eliza often asking for updates on the kids and telling her how much he wished to be with her.

Hamilton was best known as a man that never waited for others to make a move. As soon as he was nominated for the treasury he set out, that day, making his hires and readying himself and his team for the huge job that lay ahead of them.

His first assistant secretary was lifelong friend William Duer. Duer married Lady Kitty, one of Hamilton's first teenage "crushes."

This hire would prove to be a grievous hire because of the scandal Duer put the American public in during his time in the treasury office.

Hamilton had a vision of commerce alliances with countries such as Great Britain. He felt that America could create a worldwide commerce that would greatly enhance America's place in this world.

## Best Quote?

*"I am solitary lost being without you."*

*"I hate procrastination in business."*

*"I do think we are and should be great consumers."*

YOU DECIDE: **@SummaryReads**

# CHAPTER SUMMARY 16: DR. PANGLOSS
## (SUMMARY/HIGHLIGHTS & BEST QUOTES)

As Hamilton dealt with the fallout of the funding scheme of Duer, Thomas Jefferson is settling into his new position as Secretary of State. Jefferson still had some major misgivings about the new Constitution and often vacillated back and forth between opposing the governmental system and supporting it.

Eventually Jefferson chose to support the new government, but there was always a fear in the mind of Alexander Hamilton that Jefferson would turn on the Constitution and ruin everything the Federalists had worked to attain.

Hamilton and Jefferson were, possibly, the brightest minds in America during the new countries infancy. Jefferson would rise before sunrise to study. Some say he would study up to fifteen hours a day. Both were opposed to idle hands.

Many say that if the revolution had not occurred Jefferson would have never seen the light of history. His desire was to read and stay quiet. In fact it wasn't until 1791 that he took credit for the writing of the Declaration of Independence.

In 1779 Jefferson was elected Governor of Virginia. He didn't like the job and wanted to quit. He drew fire from many wishing he would take hold of the reigns of history that seemed to be following him.

## Best Quote?

*"It is wonderful how much may be done if we are always doing."*

*"It is a little cowardly to quit our posts in a bustling time."*

*"We carried Minnesota for gold are the most desperate fight on record."*

YOU DECIDE: **@SummaryReads**

# CHAPTER SUMMARY 17: THE FIRST TOWN IN AMERICA
## (SUMMARY/HIGHLIGHTS & BEST QUOTES)

As his career continued to accelerate Hamilton struggled finding a balance between the endless demands of his public life and the small changes of everyday life.

Those who were on his side felt he was a gracious, humble, and good-hearted man. While those that opposed him felt his need to always be working an angle caused him to go massively unliked. Needless to say you always felt something (positive or negative) for Alexander Hamilton.

The Hamilton's maintained a lifelong friendship with the Washington's. Eliza structured her entertaining style off of Martha and her elegant taste and perfect blend of modesty and beauty.

No matter the travel or demands placed on her husband, Eliza never complained about the effect those demands had on her and the children. She worked hard and worked often to ensure Hamilton had a wonderful place to come home to and a group of children that loved him very much.

## Best Quote?

*"Those who could speak of hiss manner from the best opportunities to observe him in public and private concurred him to be …. An open hearted gentleman…"*

*"Hamilton is an insolent coxcomb who rarely dines with*

*good company."*

*"Eliza has as much merit as your treasurer as you have as treasurer of the wealth of the United States."*

YOU DECIDE: **@SummaryReads**

# CHAPTER SUMMARY 18: OF AVARICE AND ENTERPRISE
## (SUMMARY/HIGHLIGHTS & BEST QUOTES)

December of 1790 was a monumental month for Hamilton. He presented Congress with a place for an excise tax on liquor and issued a clarion call to charter America's first central bank.

The American Revolution saw two great transformations take shape in its aftermath: The Political Revolution and the Industrial Revolution.

Hamilton worked these revolutions masterfully. Over the last two centuries his reputation has waxed and waned as his skill in the political and industrial worlds is realized more and more.

Hamilton believed that the government should promote self-fulfillment, self-improvement, and self-reliance. Washington's first term centered on economic matters that would enable these promotions.

Jefferson vastly disagreed with Hamilton. Jefferson favored the rural life for America. He distrusted the fast pace urban setting that was growing leaps and bounds in the new country. This difference of beliefs centered on the creation of a central bank. Both Adams and Jefferson strongly wanted simpler times to prevail and worked to stop Hamilton's idea for a banking system.

Adams knew that the bank was the future. So he proposed a central bank with state branches and the outlaw of private banking ventures. He would lose this battle, but be able to save face for future elections by supporting banking in some sort.

## Best Quote?

*"Hamilton was an American prophet without peer. No other founding father straddled both of these revolutions."*

*"We think of Mr. Hamilton rather than of President Washington when we look back to the policy of the first administration."*

*"Every bank in America is an enormous tax upon the people for the profit of individuals."*

YOU DECIDE: **@SummaryReads**

# CHAPTER SUMMARY 19: CITY OF THE FUTURE

## (SUMMARY/HIGHLIGHTS & BEST QUOTES)

Hamilton won the battle for a centralized bank. He was now at the height of his success. Many would relax on their success, but Hamilton knew there was a substantial minority of the country ready to come after him.

This fact should have made him more watchful of his reputation. But he was residing in Philadelphia, his family in Albany, and Philadelphia was a very sensual city in the 1700s.

With Eliza back home with the children, Hamilton falls prey to his one major vice: women. He was described in many interesting ways:

- Indelicate pleasures
- Liquorish flirtation
- Insatiable libertine

He was known as a womanizer and this would be a major issue he would have to keep quiet.

One such interlude was with a married woman, Maria Reynolds. With his family gone she would stay with him often at his home. When his wife and kids moved back to Philadelphia they had to resort to her house to keep their torrid love affair ongoing.

Maria's husband began blackmailing Hamilton to keep quiet. In the end Mr. Reynolds would invite Hamilton to his house repeatedly in an effort to get more money from Hamilton. This extortion would take years for Hamilton to reconcile.

## Best Quote?

*"The style of dress... really is an outrage upon all decency."*

*"Mr. Reynolds is not a grief-stricken husband but a shameless pimp for his wife."*

YOU DECIDE: **@SummaryReads**

# CHAPTER SUMMARY 20: CORRUPT SQUADRONS
## (SUMMARY/HIGHLIGHTS & BEST QUOTES)

Despite personal escapades and setbacks in some manufacturing ideas Hamilton still had the golden touch. Hamilton is forever marked with the idea and creation of the Bank of the United States.

But something began to brew within the southern part of the United States led by Thomas Jefferson. He knew someone had to stop the Hamiltonian juggernaut.

He knew he had to do something in the North to stop Hamilton. So he began conferring with Aaron Burr, now a New York Senator.

Jefferson and Hamilton may have been the most gifted in Washington's cabinet, but the feud was deep and it centered on two enduring visions of American government.

Jefferson struggled to force himself to fight because he was a quiet and respecting man, only fighting when he must. He employed the brash help of John Adams who was always ready for a fight.

This fight caused the beginning of the first two political parties. As Hamilton's ideals and policies took shape he became a leader of a unified and like-minded group of people that began referring to themselves as the Federalists.

The mounting fear of the impregnable power of Hamilton caused Madison and Jefferson, among others, to cohere into an organized opposition called the Republicans.

## Best Quote?

*"There is a vast mass of discontent in the South and how and when it will break God knows."*

*"I am fond of quiet, willing to do my duty, but irritable by slander and apt to be forced by it to abandon my post."*

*"Purge that constitution of its corruption...and it would be the most perfect constitution ever devised by wit of man."*

YOU DECIDE: **@SummaryReads**

# CHAPTER SUMMARY 21: EXPOSURE
## (SUMMARY/HIGHLIGHTS & BEST QUOTES)

With all the fighting and political lines being drawn, along with the past payments made to Mr. Reynolds for extra marital affairs should have made Hamilton extra vigilant about his reputation.

However, he continued his affair with Maria and continued paying hush money to Reynolds all the while risking exposure and the loss of the life he worked so hard to build.

Hamilton, a powerful man with no need to placate Madison or Jefferson, was succumbing under the power of an uneducated profligate man.

The affair came to light when Reynolds and friend, Jacob Clingman, tried to extort money from the U.S. government. The treasury department pressed charges and Hamilton allowed the whole charade to come to light.

## Best Quote?

*"I find whenever you have been with her she is cheerful and kind."*

YOU DECIDE: **@SummaryReads**

# CHAPTER SUMMARY 22: STABBED IN THE DARK

## (SUMMARY/HIGHLIGHTS & BEST QUOTES)

Jefferson and Hamilton's feud only worsened, yet they both pleaded with Washington run for a second term, knowing that he was the key to keeping the country together.

The vice presidency would be hotly contested. John Adams felt he was the only viable option for the office and felt that George Clinton posed little fight against Adams' history and superior wit.

Yet a more powerful option was rising to light, Aaron Burr. He let it be known that he was ready to speak out and allow his voice to be heard above all others. He had extensive backing and was a rising star in the political world.

The votes came in and Adams easily won the nomination with Clinton receiving enough to secure a respectable second place.

## Best Quote?

*"North and South will hang together if they have you to hang on."*

*"It is time to speak out or we are undone."*

*"If we have an embryo-Caesar in the United States 'tis Burr."*

YOU DECIDE: **@SummaryReads**

# CHAPTER SUMMARY 23: CITIZEN GENET
## (SUMMARY/HIGHLIGHTS & BEST QUOTES)

Washington's second term focused, greatly, on foreign policy. Paris was under a revolution and this was causing America to work to figure out its actual stand in the world at large.

Interestingly enough the French Revolution found solidarity in both parties. Each found their own reasons to agree or disagree with the revolution and grew with solid conviction inside their own belief systems.

Like in most circumstances no American expended more prophetic verbiage in denouncing the French Revolution than Alexander Hamilton. American apologists that ignored the cruelty of the French Revolution for their own benefit bothered Hamilton.

Another bothersome part of this saga was the news that France had declared war on England and many other countries in Europe. It appeared that war was heading straight for America.

Hamilton felt that neutrality was the only real solution to the European Wars. He fought to keep Washington focused on this idea. After days of heated fighting between Jefferson and Hamilton, President Washington issued his Proclamation of Neutrality.

## Best Quote?

*"Those mad and corrupted people in France who under the name of liberty have destroyed their own*

*government..."*

*"There seems to be no room for doubt of the existence of war."*

*"Hamilton is panic-struck if we refuse our breech to every kick which Great Britain may choose to give it."*

YOU DECIDE: **@SummaryReads**

# CHAPTER SUMMARY 24: A DISAGREEABLE TRADE
## (SUMMARY/HIGHLIGHTS)

Philadelphia was beset by a threat far more fearsome than the French minister appealing to the American people. Yellow fever swept through the northern colonies.

By late August, twenty people per day were dying from the epidemic.

Dr. Benjamin Rush was the chief medical officer taking these patients in. His treatment seems barbaric now.

- Bleed and purge the victim
- Empty the patient's bowls four times
- Drain off tem to twelve ounces of blood to lower the pulse
- Induce mild vomiting
- Do this two to three times a day

Hamilton and his wife both came down with Yellow fever. As fate would have it a childhood friend of Hamilton's arrived from the Islands. He had treated Yellow Fever for years down in the West Indies and did not believe in the barbaric approach American doctors were taking in bloodletting their patients.

- Submerge them in cold baths
- Let them drink brandy with burned cinnamon
- Sedation with opium
- Chamomile flowers, peppermint oil, and lavender sprits to help with vomiting

Edward Stevens achieved spectacular results curing the Hamilton's within five days. Hamilton used this to show the U.S. how to handle Yellow Fever. What sparked was a medical dispute between the Republicans and the Federalists. It seemed everything Hamilton and Jefferson did or believed would be debated amongst the two parties.

# CHAPTER SUMMARY 25: SEA OF BLOOD
## (SUMMARY/HIGHLIGHTS & BEST QUOTES)

As Jefferson left Washington's cabinet James Madison introduced seven congressional resolutions that made a tough anti-British trade policy. A few days later William Smith, a Federalist, released a speech of fifteen thousand words picking apart Madison's ideas. In an instance Madison knew the writer behind these words, it had to be Hamilton.

As Hamilton worked to portray England as a law-abiding ally, England did everything opposite of that. In fact England went farther than even Jefferson suggested, giving more cause to keeping England at arm's length.

When Hamilton heard about the British wrongdoings he did not behave like the British pawn he was accused of being, rather, he drew up contingency plans for President Washington to secure an army and defend coastal cities.

Hamilton wrote another letter to Washington stating that war should be a last resort. This letter remained as a focused point in foreign policy. War has been our last resort and Hamilton was the first to espouse this idea.

## Best Quote?

*"Every letter of it is Hamilton's."*

*"The English are absolute mad-men."*

*"Who but Hamilton would perfectly satisfy all our wishes?"*

YOU DECIDE: **@SummaryReads**

# CHAPTER SUMMARY 26: THE WICKED INSURGENTS OF THE WEST
## (SUMMARY/HIGHLIGHTS & BEST QUOTES)

Hamilton begins to focus on the prospect of war for America. In the end he went to war, just not with European powers, rather with American frontier settlers.

The Whiskey Rebellion in western Pennsylvania was an armed protest against the excise tax Hamilton put on alcohol. The whiskey tax was doomed to be unpopular reminding Americans of their time under British Rule.

Shortly after the whiskey tax was passed, federal collectors were shunned, tarred, feathered, blindfolded, and whipped.

Hamilton found no humor in these attacks and asked Washington to give decisive measures against these uprisings. He knew if the government did not act they would lose all control.

August 1, 6,000 rebels converged on Braddock's field outside Pittsburgh as violence took on more systematic character.

Through all the battles Washington had enough. If he states that the actions of a few will not dictate the decisions of the majority and that these lawless actions will be fought against with ferocity.

## Best Quote?

*"There is perhaps nothing so much a subject of national extravagance as these spirits."*

*"The spirit of disobedience will naturally extend and the authority of the government will prostrate."*

*"Whenever the government appears in arms, it ought to appear like Hercules and inspire respect by the display of strength."*

YOU DECIDE: **@SummaryReads**

# CHAPTER SUMMARY 27: SUGAR PLUMS AND TOYS

## (SUMMARY/HIGHLIGHTS & BEST QUOTES)

Hamilton decides to resign his position in Washington's cabinet and this ignites a nationwide debate for the young politician's future.

Governor Clinton announced he would not run for reelection, the press pegged Hamilton as the logical success for the gubernatorial seat in New York.

After his run of power it was clear that Hamilton had a vice, power. He didn't extort his power for money and when he left office he desperately needed money more than he did upon his American arrival decades earlier.

Hamilton earned $3,500 a years as Secretary of the Treasury, far less than he needed to earn caring for a family of 8 children.

Hamilton grew up with no security and wanted to create a secure life for his family, however, he refused to do this with any venture below board. He would earn his money the right and hard way.

He jumped back into law and began working in New York as a preeminent lawyer.

## Best Quote?

*"I got to take a little care of my own, which need my care not a little."*

YOU DECIDE: **@SummaryReads**

# CHAPTER SUMMARY 28: SPARE CASSIUS
## (SUMMARY/HIGHLIGHTS & BEST QUOTES)

Hamilton was more than the principal theorists of the Federalists. He was the chief tactician, organizer, and mobilizing the faithful through letters, speeches, and writings. This continued in the private sector and so did the demands of his law office.

Months after leaving office he wrote to his national bank and admitted he lost his bankbook and did not know his account balance. He was beginning to be absent minded, not undue to the mental stress he always placed upon himself.

He wanted to travel, but never left the northern states after his arrival. His enormous workload must have assisted in this lack of international travel by such a powerful statesman.

## Best Quote?

*"I am overwhelmed in professional business and have scarcely a moment for anything else."*

*"He was employed in every important and every commercial case."*

YOU DECIDE: **@SummaryReads**

# CHAPTER SUMMARY 29: THE MAN IN THE GLASS BUBBLE

## (SUMMARY/HIGHLIGHTS & BEST QUOTES)

During the quest for independence, John Adams, was the most passionate voice for war with Great Britain.

He was considered a difficult and perplexing man that did not have the social graces other founding fathers prevailed with. Still he was successful in his approach and a leader in the foundation of America.

## Best Quote?

*"He cannot dance, drink, game, flatter, promise, dress, swear with gentlemen, and talk small talk or flirt with the ladies."*

YOU DECIDE: **@SummaryReads**

# CHAPTER SUMMARY 30: FLYING TOO NEAR THE SUN

## (SUMMARY/HIGHLIGHTS & BEST QUOTES)

At age 42 Hamilton receives a letter from William Hamilton, his uncle. Hamilton had no contact with his paternal family up until this letter. It brought him great satisfaction.

Hamilton's return letter was vague, at best, about his life story but did allow his uncle to learn the truth about his father. He stated his father's troubles and the separation and that his father still lived in the West Indies and that all pleas to come north and live with his son were met with no response.

Hamilton remembered that these Scottish born Hamilton's never came to his rescue when he was an impoverished boy living in the islands. In fact his uncle wrote to him for selfish reasons. His business had gone down and needed to lean on the eminence of his American nephew. This did not deter Alexander from making the connection to his father's family.

## Best Quote?

*"I have strongly pressed the old gentleman to come to reside with me."*

YOU DECIDE: **@SummaryReads**

# CHAPTER SUMMARY 31: AN INSTRUMENT OF HELL

## (SUMMARY/HIGHLIGHTS & BEST QUOTES)

The chief reason Hamilton feared the repercussions of the Reynolds affairs was the if America went to war with France, he wanted in as a major piece of the solution and such a scandal would sink his chances.

President Adams devised a two-part strategy against France:

- Maintain American neutrality through negotiations
- Expand military in case talks miscarried

The secretaries of state, war, and treasury all wrote to Hamilton for his guidance, never allowing President Adams to know. He never denigrated Adams, but offered good advice and worked to believe the executive office was in good hands.

On the contrary, Vice President Jefferson was working to weaken the view of the president in French eyes. Jefferson predicted that Adams would last one term and that the French should invade England.

## Best Quote?

*"I believe there is no danger of want of firmness in the executive."*

*"Mr. Adams is vain, suspicious, and stubborn, of an excessive regard, taking counsel with nobody."*

# CHAPTER SUMMARY 32: REIGN OF WITCHES
## (SUMMARY/HIGHLIGHTS & BEST QUOTES)

President Adams time in office can be described as political savagery with few historical parallels in American history.

In 1798 Congress enacted four famous laws designed to muzzle dissent and browbeat the Republicans into submission:

- Alien and Sedition Act
- The Naturalization Act
- The Alien Enemies Act
- Sedition Act

The Federalist controlled congress was maneuvering for partisan advantage and wanted to hinder the Republican movement.

## Best Quote?

*"Jeffersonians are more Frenchmen than Americans."*

*"A more careful and attentive watch out to be kept over foreigners."*

*"But like Caesar, you are ambition and for that ambition to enslave his country."*

YOU DECIDE: @SummaryReads

# CHAPTER SUMMARY 33: WORKS GODLY AND UNGODLY

## (SUMMARY/HIGHLIGHTS & BEST QUOTES)

In 1799 the New York Manumission Society voted to abolish slavery in the state of New York. This was to be gradual, but it caused Aaron Burr to move over to the Federalist majority at the time.

Alexander Hamilton largely sorted the Federalist anti-slavery movement. At the same time Eliza carried out her own activism helping the marginal and downtrodden.

Eliza was never allowed to forget the Reynolds's affair her husband had for many years. The Republican Party worked diligently to keep it in the public's memory every chance they got.

Hamilton, now in his mid-forties, was appointed inspector general and bore the weight of the entire army while still working in the private sector.

Dr. Joseph Browne attacks the water system of New York saying the contamination from the river causes yearly outbreaks of Yellow Fever. He suggests creating a private water corporation.

This was actually a big ruse by Aaron Burr to get a Republican Bank into New York and he accomplished the task by getting three Federalist on his side, including Alexander Hamilton.

He never let Hamilton in on his overreaching plan and during the final prep for the vote Burr changed a few details in the proposition, making it legal for the water company to open up as a money lending source.

## Best Quote?

*"No member of the committee of six worked harder than Hamilton to make possible Aaron Burr's upcoming triumph in the New York legislature."*

YOU DECIDE: **@SummaryReads**

# CHAPTER SUMMARY 34: IN AN EVIL HOUR
## (SUMMARY/HIGHLIGHTS & BEST QUOTES)

Theodore Sedgwick, Speaker of the House, asks whether the newly acquired Washington should be given the title General in the army.

Washington had been asked back to direct the army and now his title was yet to be determined. Adams throws a temper tantrum; think Sedgwick is trying to get Washington back into the White House to lead the country.

Sedgwick's question was as innocuous as it sounded and it meant to harm to Adams. However, this caused a larger separation from the Federalists (Sedgwick was a member) and the Republican Party.

President Adams is driven to make more, seemingly, mad requests that cause both parties to distance themselves from the second president.

## Best Quote?

*"What, are you going to appoint him general over the president?"*

YOU DECIDE: **@SummaryReads**

# CHAPTER SUMMARY 35: GUSTS OF PASSION
## (SUMMARY/HIGHLIGHTS & BEST QUOTES)

Burr and Hamilton's, again, paths crossed this time in the private sector. Both men were brought together to defend a man suspected of murdering his fiancé.

Many wonder why these two men decided to work together, after Burr's trickery with the private water company, and the answer can be found in politics. This was a highly followed murder trial and both men needed to look good in the public's eye to help with local elections taking place that would have a profound effect on the national scene.

The trial was unfolding with incredible speed. Fifty-five witnesses testified in only three days. Hamilton became legendary again when he placed two candles on the sides of the face of Richard Croucher while he testified.

This caused Croucher, the real killer, to look and sound ominous to the point he confessed in the witness chair. Later on Aaron Burr tried to take credit for the candle idea.

The defendant was declared not guilty in less than five minutes and the chief counsel on the prosecution side came over and threatened Alexander Hamilton claiming that he should die before natural causes. Unbeknownst to her, Hamilton stood beside his eventual killer in Aaron Burr.

## Best Quote?

*"He appeared as white as ashes and trembled all over like a leaf."*

*"The jury will mark every muscle of his face, every motion of his eye."*

*"Behold the murderer, gentlemen!"*

*"If thee dies a natural death, I shall think there is no justice in heaven."*

YOU DECIDE: **@SummaryReads**

# CHAPTER SUMMARY 36: IN A VERY BELLIGERENT HUMOR

## (SUMMARY/HIGHLIGHTS & BEST QUOTES)

Hamilton struggled to ignore those that spurned him. Vendettas were something he couldn't easily pass up. In fact he would brood for a time over an issue and that take to vicious attacks with the pen.

One such attack was in the form of private Federalist papers he wrote on President John Adams. He never intended those to go public but eventually they did and proved to be sensational in the public's eye. Historians believe that Aaron Burr discovered the letters and provided newspaper with the salacious writing.

Jefferson and Hamilton always seemed to be on differing sides of the political debate. Jefferson maintained his distrust of the government while Hamilton distrusted those being governed.

## Best Quote?

*"Hamilton looked at the world through a dark filter and had a better sense of human limitations."*

*"Jefferson viewed the world through a rose-colored prism and had a better sense of human potentialities."*

YOU DECIDE: @SummaryReads

# CHAPTER SUMMARY 37: DEADLOCK
## (SUMMARY/HIGHLIGHTS & BEST QUOTES)

President Adams was finally able to sign a peace treaty with France. Though America never went to official war with their former ally the public grew tired of the threatening clouds of a French and American war.

As a new election was beginning to take place it pitted two of Hamilton's most long running foes: Jefferson and Burr. Feeling that one would win the presidency he decided to pick the lesser of the two evils and throw his support to Thomas Jefferson.

If forced to choose, Hamilton would choose a man with wrong principles, Jefferson, opposed to one with none, Burr.

## Best Quote?

*"The Federal Administration steered the vessel through all the storms raised by Europe into a peaceable and safe port."*

*"Jefferson is by far not so dangerous a man and he has pretensions to character."*

*"Burr is far more cunning than wise, far more dexterous than able. In my opinion he is inferior in real ability to Jefferson."*

*"The appointment of Burr as president would disgrace our country abroad."*

YOU DECIDE: **@SummaryReads**

# CHAPTER SUMMARY 38: A WORLD FULL OF FOLLY

## (SUMMARY/HIGHLIGHTS & BEST QUOTES)

Once Jefferson became president, Hamilton, forty-six, began to fade from public view. He and Eliza decided to build their dream house.

They built it in New York on a nice farm and named it The Grange, a name his father had for his farm in the British West Indies.

Hamilton through his whole soul into building this piece of property, he would study other homes and take ideas from far off places and mold them into something that would make the Hamilton manor unique.

Burr, who betrayed Jefferson's trust, was Jefferson's vice-president during his first term. Was excluded from any presidential council meetings and abruptly replaced in the next election.

Jefferson endowed his election with cosmic significance. He stated it was a revolution of governmental principles much like the revolution of 1776. Jefferson, history tells us, was a much more moderate president than either he or Hamilton would ever admit.

## Best Quote?

*"A disappointed politician is very apt to take refuge in a garden."*

*"We are told and we believe that Jefferson and Burr hate each other and Hamilton thinks Jefferson is too cunning to be outwitted by him."*

YOU DECIDE: **@SummaryReads**

# CHAPTER SUMMARY 39: PAMPHLET WARS
## (SUMMARY/HIGHLIGHTS & BEST QUOTES)

Political ideology was evolving and Jefferson evolved with it. He cultivated rapport with the common man while Hamilton stayed in the outdated paternalistic view of politics.

Hamilton writes a letter mourning the death of his son and talks about how he has devoted his life to the Constitution and now it all seems to be worthless.

Hamilton began to realize that the Federalist relied too much on reason while the Republicans focused on emotion. So he began writing pamphlets that strongly brought together God, the Constitution, and the Federalist Party. He hoped to bring down Thomas Jefferson through evoking emotion in the common man.

## Best Quote?

*"The Federalists found themselves on the wrong side of a historical divide."*

*"Men are rather reasoning than reasonable animals, for the most part governed by their passion."*

*"By signing up God against Thomas Jefferson, Hamilton hoped to make a more potent political appeal."*

YOU DECIDE: **@SummaryReads**

# CHAPTER SUMMARY 40: THE PRICE OF TRUTH
## (SUMMARY/HIGHLIGHTS & BEST QUOTES)

Alexander Hamilton seemed to have massive inner conflict in his later years. After his loss to Jefferson he seemed to vacillate between wanting to leave public life and retire to the country and live a life consumed with his political future.

As he, once again, was back in the private sector he concentrated on law and political theory rather than everyday politics. A publisher wanted to publish *The Federalist Papers* and he balked at the project before finally deciding in favor of the submission.

He would take on cases that directly had to do with Jefferson's politics ensure the president would have to respond.

Jefferson would free Republicans jailed from the Sedition Act and exact revenge against Federalists in the same camp. One such Federalist was Harry Croswell. He took to attacking Jefferson in print and, upon arrest, desired to be defended by Alexander Hamilton.

Hamilton could not defend the man and bound by the exact letter of the law the jurors had to find Croswell guilty.

## Best Quote?

*"Put that paper in your pocket, Baron."*

*"To lash the rascals naked through the world…"*

YOU DECIDE: **@SummaryReads**

# CHAPTER SUMMARY 41: A DESPICABLE OPINION
## (SUMMARY/HIGHLIGHTS & BEST QUOTES)

In 1804 Hamilton speaks with Judge John Tyler about the, seemingly, awful prognosis of Aaron Burr as governor. This private dinner triggers a chain of events that lead to the duel with Burr.

At the dinner was Charles D. Cooper who sat back and listened to the Federalists talk gravely about Burr. He reported it to Andrew Brown and before long the letter he wrote to Brown appeared in the New-York Evening Post.

Burr lost the election and upon reading the letters published in the Post went into a fit of rage. During his tie with Jefferson for president in 1801 Hamilton called Burr:

- Profligate
- Bankrupt
- Corrupt
- Unprincipled

The political fight was beginning to get personal and Burr had enough. Now that Hamilton was not protected by Washington or Adams and now that Burr's political career was over he would not need to stand idly aside and let his name be drug through the mud.

A duel with Hamilton would bring back the honor Burr's name had lost. By the next morning Burr had cultivated a letter to Hamilton demanding him give an account for his malicious behavior and slanderous tone he had taken against Burr.

After his response Burr challenged Hamilton to a duel.

Though duels were not so commonplace in American folklore at the time, they were common for military men and these two men both had military backgrounds.

As he accepted the duel he admitted going against his own ideals for the cause of public opinion. Hamilton began sharing with close friends that he would waste his shot and not try to attack Burr. Many felt this was a way to end his life and his depression that had plagued him for years.

Hamilton also felt that Burr would not shoot to kill and that Burr knew no benefit would come from murdering Hamilton. Upon hearing Burr had every intention of murder Hamilton still refused to take aim.

## Best Quote?

*"Burr is a dangerous man and one who ought not to be trusted."*

*"Burr was a man with a wounded reputation."*

*"Hamilton was obsessed with dueling in the abstract, but not with duels in fact."*

*"Instead of killing Burr he invited Burr to kill him."*

*"Then, sir, you will go like a lamb to be slaughtered."*

YOU DECIDE: @SummaryReads

# CHAPTER SUMMARY 42: FATAL ERRAND
## (SUMMARY/HIGHLIGHTS & BEST QUOTES)

As the duel came close Hamilton seemed fixated on the fact that he would die. He spent his last weekend at The Grange with his wife and kids. He spent his last evening finishing work and paying off his final debtor so that Eliza would have nothing to worry about.

As the men fired it appeared that Burr fired first and that Hamilton only fired as a reflected muscle movement from being hit.

Hamilton fell to the ground and immediately declared the he was a dead man.

## Best Quote?

*"I pray God that something may remain for the maintenance and education of my dear wife and children."*

*"I am a dead man."*

YOU DECIDE: @SummaryReads

# CHAPTER SUMMARY 43: THE MELTING SCENE

## (SUMMARY/HIGHLIGHTS & BEST QUOTES)

Because of his youth, his political service, and his woeful end, Hamilton received what he never got in life, an emotional outpouring of sympathy.

New York mourned as it lost its most distinguished citizen.

**Best Quote?**

*"Streets crowded with those who carry badges of mourning because the first of their fellow citizens has sunk in blood."*

YOU DECIDE: **@SummaryReads**

# Concluding Analysis

There is no doubt that Alexander Hamilton was a major force in the countries beginning and in forming the tone and nature of the constitution that established a strong Federal government (at the expense of the relative independence the states enjoyed prior to its ratification) and this is clearly laid out in Chernow's groundbreaking book.

Reading through the reviews of Chernow's book show that even critics find very little to criticize and we also enjoyed reading and summarizing his work that still is still on the best-seller list after all these years.

We hope you have a sense of his book and that we have been able to save you some of the most valuable resource you have, namely your time.

Remember...

**INTEREST – TIME = SUMMARY READS!**

# FURTHER READING

Are you ready to quickly absorb the main points and highlights of the next best seller? Check out the other great summaries from *Summary Reads*:

■ Karl Rove's latest book, ***The Triumph of William McKinley: Why the Election of 1896 Still Matters*** is a great read, but it is a LONG book. We have already read it and summarized it for you so pick up a copy and enjoy:

http://amzn.com/B018Y0POJY

■ Brian Kilmeade's latest best-seller, ***Thomas Jefferson and the Tripoli Pirates,*** is a fascinating story about a forgotten war. Get the summary today:

http://amzn.com/B018B8FFWK

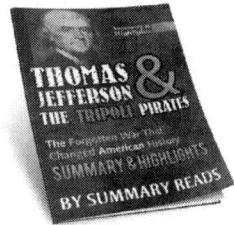

■ Crippled America is Trump's latest book and we have the top summary on the market:

http://amzn.com/B017QT0IMM

■ The over 900 page best-seller ***Destiny and Power*** is a great book but not everyone has the time for the whole book. Check out our summary and save hours: http://amzn.com/B019D70GI6

Last but **DEFINITELY NOT LEAST** is our best-seller summary of Mary Beard's *SPQR: A History of Ancient Rome.*

Get your copy today:   http://amzn.com/B018MANYA2

# FREE GIFT SPECIAL REPORT

## The 10 Strange Deaths of Vladimir Putin

While History is filled with intrigue, war posturing, bribes and assassinations our current day is just as filled (if not more) with exciting (if not terrifying) but true stories.

As our **free gift** for being a **SUMMARY READS enthusiast** we are happy to give you a special report about some of the mysterious and strange deaths that have befallen Mr. Putin's enemies.

Plane crashes, multiple stab wounds and radioactive sushi are just a few of the misfortunes that have befallen those who opposed the Russian President.

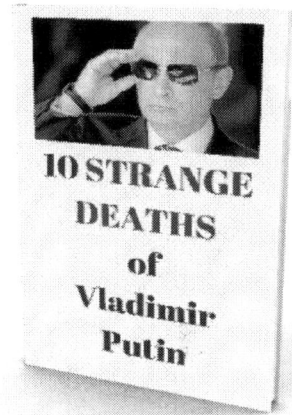

10 STRANGE DEATHS of Vladimir Putin

Get your free copy at:

## http://sixfigureteen.com/summaryreads

ALSO: We will let you know about future Summary Reads titles so this is win-win! Enjoy your FREE GIFT and thank you for being part of the SUMMARY READS Family!